Mythical Beasts

MYTHICAL CREATURES AROUND THE WORLD

By Joanne Rippin

Cavendish Square

Published in 2023 by Cavendish Square Publishing, LLC
2544 Clinton Street, Buffalo, NY 14224

Originally Published in English by Haynes Publishing under the title: *Mythical Beasts Pocket Manual* © Haynes Publishing 2020

Website: cavendishsq.com

Design and layout by Richard Parsons
Thanks to the following agencies for use of their images:
Alamy; (cover) pp 9, 12, 17, 25, 29. **Bridgeman Art Library**. **Getty**. **Shutterstock** Grom08 (cover).

Cataloging-in-Publication Data

Names: Rippin, Joanne.
Title: Mythical creatures around the world / Joanne Rippin.
Description: New York : Cavendish Square Publishing, 2023. | Series: Mythical beasts |
Includes glossary and index.
Identifiers: ISBN 9781502667366 (pbk.) | ISBN 9781502667373 (library bound) |
ISBN 9781502667380 (ebook)
Subjects: LCSH: Animals, Mythical--Juvenile literature. | Mythology--Juvenile literature.
Classification: LCC GR825.R577 2023 | DDC 398.24'54--dc23

CPSIA compliance information: Batch #CWCSQ23: For further information contact Cavendish Square Publishing LLC at 1-877-980-4450.

Printed in the United States of America

The Author

Joanne is an experienced writer and editor, who has published many historical books on a wide variety of subjects. She has a long-standing fascination with mythical creatures, and has a dog who thinks it's half human.

Contents

Centaur	4
Dragon	8
Gorgon	12
Qilin	16
Tengu	20
Troll	24
Unicorn	28
Glossary	32
For More Information	32
Index	32

CENTAUR
HALF HORSE AND HALF MAN

According to Greek mythology, centaurs were part human, part horse. They were the descendants of Centaurus, who was the son of a man named Ixion and a cloud nymph named Nephele. Centaurus was unhappy living with humans and went to live with herds of wild horses on Mount Pelion. His children had the head, arms, and chest of a human, but the lower half of a horse.

Forces of Nature

Centaurs were said to live in family groups in the wilds of Thessaly. They had a reputation for riotous behavior and fierce fighting (with each other as well as with humans), especially after drinking too much wine. They were usually shown as followers of Dionysus, the Greek god of wine, and in stories they were often used to represent the dark, uncontrollable forces of nature. Centaurs also appear in Roman legends as well as in modern literature.

Did you know?

After Chiron died, the gods honored him by placing him among the stars as a constellation, where he became known as Centaurus or Sagittarius.

CHIRON AND FIRENZE

A few centaurs were wise and noble. The most famous of these is Chiron, who was loved and respected by everyone for his learning and healing skills. Chiron was fostered by the god Apollo, who taught him that learning music, medicine, archery, and other human skills would help him rise above his animal nature.

Chiron became the ruler of all the centaurs as well as a tutor to Greek heroes, including Heracles, Achilles, and Jason. He also taught Asclepius, the famous doctor, about surgery, potions, and the use of drugs.

Apollo *Chiron* *Asclepius*

Known Facts

Name:	Centaur
Family status:	Originally the offspring of a human man and female horse
Career:	Living wild and free in the mountains, with frequent parties
Personality:	With a few exceptions, wild and rude, prone to fighting
Appearance:	Head, arms, and chest of a human; legs, body, and tail of a horse
Symbols:	Bow and arrow, laurel wreath, wine

Worst-ever wedding guests

One of the most famous stories of how badly behaved centaurs can be takes place at a royal wedding party, where they had been invited as guests by the king. The centaurs got so drunk that they rioted, had a huge fight, and then ran off with the bride!

DRAGON

FIRE-BREATHING AND FABULOUS

Dragons are amazing. They have been part of human myths, legends, and stories for thousands of years, all over the world. There are many different types of dragons, including the cosmic dragon (source of earth and sky), the Chinese dragon (emperor of earth, sea, and sky), the Indian and Ethiopian dragon (creature of marsh and mountain), and the Western dragon (fire-breathing terror of the skies).

LEGENDARY DRAGONS

In many stories, a dragon is the traditional enemy of knights and heroes. All around the world, there are tales of brave men on horseback saving towns, villages, tied-up maidens, and treasure hoards from fire-breathing dragons. Dragons have also featured in J. R. R. Tolkien's book *The Hobbit* and in Cressida Cowell's book *How to Train Your Dragon*. In some media, dragons are huge, terrifying, and would be very difficult for a knight in metal armor on a panicking horse to kill with a spear and a sword. In other media, dragons are mysterious, wise, and even friendly. Some—like those in Patricia C. Wrede's Enchanted Forest books—can talk and have their own unique personalities.

St. George

Did you know?

Asian dragons are very different from European dragons. In China, Japan, and Korea, dragons are generally kind, in spite of their frightening appearance and demonic eyes. They tend not to have wings; instead, they fly by magic and always have four legs.

Creature of the World

The word "dragon" comes from the Greek *drakōn*, which means "snake." The first dragons in classical mythology were more like huge snakes with legs, often guarding treasure. Roman dragons were the first to have wings and breathe fire, while the dragons in the myths of Babylon are hybrid creatures—small and slender, with a snake's scaly body, the legs of a lion, and a scorpion's tail. Largest of all Earth dragons, Indian dragons grow to a length of 180 feet (55 m). They have a mystical gem in their forehead that cures all diseases, golden scales, a bushy beard, and a tall crest on the forehead.

Known Facts

Name:	Dragon
Family status:	Live in almost every culture; hatch from eggs
Career:	Guard treasure, terrorize neighborhoods, steal maidens; some can be tamed or befriended
Personality:	Almost always fierce and bad-tempered, but sometimes kind and wise
Appearance:	Varies from small snake with legs to huge, winged, fire-breathing reptile
Symbolizes:	Anger, greed, and envy in the West; power, strength, and luck in the East

Pendragon

King Arthur was known as the Pendragon. In Welsh, *pen* means "chief." In medieval times, a dragon was often used on battle banners, and a red dragon is still used on the Welsh flag.

GORGON

VICIOUS SISTERS OR FEMINIST ICONS

In the earliest of Greek legends, there was only one gorgon. However, Homer later said there were three, named Stheno, Euryale, and Medusa. They were the daughters of the sea god Phorcys and his sister-wife Ceto. Another tradition says that the gorgon was created by Gaia—the Earth goddess and mother of everything—to help her sons fight the gods. Later stories say that the third gorgon, Medusa, was born a beautiful mortal woman who attracted the attention of Poseidon, the sea god. One day, he found Medusa alone and forced himself on her in a temple dedicated to Athena. Furious at this desecration of her sacred space, Athena changed Medusa's beautiful hair into snakes and gave her a face so awful that anyone who looked at her was turned to stone.

Medusa in the film Clash of the Titans.

Gorgon Appearance

The earliest pictures of gorgons are paintings on classical Greek pottery. They have a female human form but with wings; a scaly body; broad, round heads; staring eyes; and open mouths with tongues sticking out. They sometimes have tusks, and their hair is made out of living snakes. Legend said that blood taken from a gorgon's right side could bring a dead person back to life, but blood from the left was an instantly fatal poison.

Did you know?

The image of Medusa's severed head was used for centuries as a symbol of protection and was carved on the gateways and doors of buildings to ward off evil.

MEDUSA

Although she was born from the same parents as her gorgon sisters, Medusa was mortal and looked like a human until Athena blamed her for being attacked. Medusa is most famous for being killed by Perseus, who was ordered by King Polydectes to bring back the gorgon's head. To avoid being turned into stone, Perseus cut off Medusa's head while she was sleeping. He used his shield as a mirror so he wouldn't accidentally be turned to stone.

When Medusa was killed, she was pregnant, and her two children sprang from her neck. One of them was Pegasus, an immortal winged horse. An ancient Greek poet named Pindar wrote that when the Gorgons realized their sister was dead, they cried for her. Athena heard them and made a musical instrument called the aulos that sounded just like them.

Known Facts

Name: Gorgon

Family status: Daughters of Phorcys and Ceto

Career: Lived in an isolated area of Libya, hidden away from mortals

Personality: Kept to themselves, but if attacked could defend themselves with poisonous blood and a deadly gaze

Appearance: Female form, with wings and snakes for hair

Symbolizes: Protection in early times; later on, female power

Female power

Some scholars think that the gorgons were symbols of women's power and wisdom. Their staring eyes symbolize the ability to see through illusions and find the truth, and their snake hair represents the cycle of birth, death, and renewal.

QILIN

GENTLE, HORNED HYBRID

Also known in Japan as the Kylin, the Chinese Qilin is a strange creature of many parts. It has the head of an eastern dragon, a single horn on its forehead, a yellow belly, a multicolored or golden back, the hooves of a horse, the body and antlers of a deer, and the tail of an ox. Some descriptions say it has dragon scales on its body.

DEATH AND THE QILIN

The Qilin is hardly ever seen by humans, and at the rare times when it is, its appearance often coincides with the imminent birth or death of a wise person (known as a "sage" in China) or a great ruler. There are legends that say a Qilin appeared before the birth and the death of the great philosopher Confucius. Its name is a combination of the Chinese characters *qi*, meaning "male," and *lin,* meaning "female."

方楚欽
馬淑娟

Protectors of good people

Although gentle and peaceful, Qilin can breathe fire, like dragons. This happens when they get angry, and they only get angry when a good and virtuous person is threatened or mistreated by a malicious one.

Wise Vegetarians

In Buddhist traditions, Qilin are said to refuse to walk on grass in case they damage it or accidentally kill a tiny creature, so they are often shown in paintings walking on clouds or the water. As heavenly and peaceful creatures, they also refuse to eat meat. They are said to be able to tell if an accused person is guilty of a crime or not, and there are several ancient stories of court trials where a Qilin makes the final judgement.

Qilin statues are very common in China. This one is at the entrance of the Imperial Palace in Beijing.

Known Facts

Name: Qilin or Kylin

Family status: Qilin live in heaven, and their ancestry isn't known

Career: Appearing before the birth or death of a wise person or leader

Personality: Wise, virtuous, gentle

Appearance: Dragon-like head with antlers, multicolored body, tail and hooves of an ox

Symbolizes: Luck, protection, success

Did you know?

Sometimes the Qilin is called the Chinese unicorn, but it doesn't really look like a unicorn at all apart from the horn on its forehead.

TENGU

A POWERFUL JAPANESE DEMON

Japan's ancient spirit world is full of fabulous demons and supernatural beings called *yōkai*. Tengu are yōkai who are a bit like modern comic book heroes: they can fly, are incredibly strong, and have magical powers and impressive martial arts skills. Like a lot of yōkai, the tengu started off as animals. One version of the tengu, called kotengu, are still sometimes shown as creatures with the head of a bird. More often, though, they have an angry red face and a long nose that is thought to be a kind of humanized version of a beak. Tengu are often shown holding huge fans made of feathers. In some folktales, these fans are said to have the power to grow or shrink a human's nose, but in others, they are what the tengu use to control the wind.

Trickster Demon

Although the tengu have had different characteristics and appearances through the centuries, they have always been good at playing tricks. When they first appeared in folktales in the 9th and 10th centuries, they weren't very powerful at all. They were limited to starting small fires, throwing stones, and sometimes possessing farm workers for a while. By the 11th century, however, they were less easy to defeat and were enemies of Buddhists. In the 14th century, they were shown with red faces and a long nose, and they began to develop superhero powers—including the ability to fly and control the weather. Often, the tengu are angry, as their fierce red faces suggest, but they can also be good, acting as guardians of the forests and protecting places such as temples (as long as they aren't Buddhist).

Tengu parades

Tengu are very popular characters at festivals and parades in Japan, and their masks are sold in shops all over the country. A distinctive part of the costume is the shoes, called *tengu geta*. They are made from blocks of wood with a flip-flop style strap on top, and it takes a lot of practice to be able to walk in them.

Enemies of Buddhism

Buddhist teachers have always said that the tengu are disruptive and evil demons who cause war and kidnap children. In some stories, the Tengu tease Buddhist priests, lead them to the wrong roads when they are traveling, rob temples of their treasures, and sometimes even impersonate the monks or nuns.

Known Facts

Name:	Tengu
Family status:	Demon
Career:	Good fighters; can control weather and enjoy playing tricks on Buddhist monks
Personality:	Sometimes harmless and protective, sometimes naughty, often fierce and angry
Appearance:	Tall human figure with a red face and long nose; sometimes has the head of a raven and black wings
Symbols:	Birds of prey, fan of feathers, long red nose

Did you know?

There is a tengu emoji! It has the red, angry face and long nose of a tengu, and is called "Japanese goblin."

TROLL

STRANGE, UGLY CREATURES

Trolls can come in several shapes and sizes. In northern European traditions, they are stomping giants who eat humans. There are also human-size or smaller trolls who live in the wilderness, often underground or in caves. In Scandinavian tales, trolls are generally large, brutal, and ugly. They have horns, warts, green skin, and oversized ears and noses. They live in castles rather than caves. Trolls are often said to be a bit on the dim side, although they can be clever when it comes to stealing treasure or human children. The word "troll" comes from an Old Norse word that means "magic."

OGRE

In French and English fairy tales, an ogre is very similar to a Scandinavian troll. They are giant beings with an oversized head, large stomach, and long hair. Like trolls, they enjoy eating humans—especially children—are very strong, and aren't very bright. Perhaps the most famous ogre couple in recent times is Shrek and Fiona, stars of the Shrek movies from DreamWorks Pictures. In legends, ogres are not as friendly as these two.

Troll dolls

In 1959, a Danish fisherman and woodcutter named Thomas Dam couldn't afford a Christmas present for his daughter, so he carved a little troll-shaped doll for her. When all her school friends also wanted a little troll doll, he began selling them. Eventually, he started a company called Dam Things to make them out of plastic instead of wood.

Miniature Trolls

The Shetland and Orkney islands, in the far north of Scotland, were once ruled by Norse kings. Here, trolls are called trows. They are very different from their giant relatives and are said to be small creatures who live in dirt mounds or near the sea. They are rarely seen, as they only appear at night, and there aren't many descriptions. Most say they could pass for very old, ugly little humans. Like the larger trolls, stories say they sometimes carry off human children. Some stories claim that trows will sneak into a house when the owners are in bed and warm themselves by the dying fire. Their barrows are said to be full of treasure because they are good at making things out of precious metals such as silver and gold.

Known Facts

Name:	Troll, ogre, or trow
Family status:	Live in family groups and have troll children
Career:	Remain hidden from humans, often living in caves or underground
Personality:	Not very intelligent; some are destructive and evil, others just like a quiet life
Appearance:	Varied, but always ugly
Symbols:	Club, cave, wild hair

Did you know?

Troll dolls have become movie stars, first in *Toy Story* (Disney/Pixar, 1995) and then in their very own movie *Trolls* (DreamWorks, 2016).

UNICORN

MAGICAL HORSE WITH A HORN

The first description of a unicorn was by the Greek doctor Ctesias in the 4th century BCE. He called this creature a *monokerōs*, or "single-horn" (in Latin, *unicornis*), and said that this wild donkey from India was the size of a small horse, with a white body, a purple head, and blue eyes. On its forehead was a long horn colored red at the pointed tip, black in the middle, and white at the base. He said that its horn could purify water and protect people from epilepsy and poison. The *monokerōs* could gallop very fast and was difficult to capture. It would fight anyone who tried.

UNICORNS IN HISTORY

The idea of the unicorn has captured the imaginations and hearts of people for years, and in many parts of the world, people believed they were real animals. In medieval times, it was said that unicorns were shy and could only be tamed by young maidens. Musicians and storytellers made the unicorn a symbol of courtly love in their tales of knights and ladies.

Did you know?

In the 15th century, unicorns became a popular symbol in heraldry. The royal coat of arms of the United Kingdom features a lion, representing England, and a unicorn, representing Scotland.

MODERN UNICORNS

In the 16th and 17th centuries, people still believed that unicorns were real. For awhile, people sold medicine that they claimed was made out of ground unicorn horns. In reality, it was made from narwhal horns or the tusks of elephants. However, unicorns have remained popular even after people realized they aren't real. A book called *The Last Unicorn*, written by Peter S. Beagle in 1968, is still a favorite with people of all ages today. Unicorns can be found in books, movies, comics, toys, blankets, notebooks, and much more.

That's quite a success story for a mythical beast—to be known and loved all over the world for nearly 2,500 years!

Known Facts

Name:	Unicorn
Family status:	Naturally born to other unicorns
Career:	Hides in quiet forest glades; has magical qualities
Personality:	Shy, gentle, and wise
Appearance:	About the size of a pony, often pure white, single horn on its forehead. Modern unicorns come in every color.
Symbolizes:	Purity, protection, rarity, magic

A herd of unicorns

Marco Polo, the Italian explorer from the 13th century, said he had seen a herd of unicorns on his travels. He was disappointed and said they were ugly creatures, not at all as lovely as he'd been led to believe. This is because they were actually rhinoceroses.

Glossary

coincide: To happen at the same time.

desecrate: To treat a sacred place or sacred object shamefully or with great disrespect.

foster: To give parental care even though not related by blood or legal ties

heraldry: The practice of tracing and recording family history and creating coats of arms.

hybrid: Something that is made up of two or more different things.

imminent: Just about to happen.

malicious: Feeling or showing a desire to cause harm to another person.

For More Information

Krensky, Stephen, and Pham Quan Phuc. *The Book of Mythical Beasts and Magical Creatures.* London, UK: DK, 2020.

CBC: *https://www.cbc.ca/kids/quizzes/personality-quiz-mythical-creatures.*

Index

blood, 13, 15

China, 8, 10, 16, 18, 19

demons, 10, 20, 21, 22, 23

fire, 8, 10, 11, 18, 21, 26

Greece, 4, 5, 6, 11, 12, 13, 14, 28

India, 8, 10, 28

Japan, 10, 16, 20, 22, 23

movies, 25, 27, 30

protection, 14, 15, 18, 19, 21, 23, 28, 31

treasure, 8, 10, 11, 22, 24, 26